brave new girl

brave new girl

HOW TO BE FEARLESS

LOU HAMILTON

Published by Sourcebooks, Inc.
P.O. Box 4410, Naperville, Illinois 60567-4410
(630) 961-3900
Fax: (630) 961-2168
www.sourcebooks.com

Originally published as *Brave New Girl* in 2016 in the United Kingdom by Orion Spring, an imprint of the Orion Publishing Group, Ltd.

Printed and bound in China.
LEO 10 9 8 7 6 5 4 3 2 1

To my son, Solomon,
for your positive presence and fearless energy.

~

To my daughter, Ruby May,
for your guiding light and fun-loving spirit.

~

To my Granny May,
for sending down the drawings from wherever you are.

Contents

Introduction   viii

1   Aim for the moon   1

2   Face your fears   25

3   Be your own superhero   47

4   Your time will come   73

5   Reinvent the uphill struggle   97

6   Look for magic   117

7   Frivolity is freedom   143

8   Take a break   159

9   Work together to achieve great things   177

10 You're good enough   207

Acknowledgments   227

About the author   229

Introduction

When my daughter, Ruby May, was leaving school and heading out into the world, I must admit I felt a little fearful. Letting go is scary for a mom, but I was determined not to hold her back with my own fears. In fact, I wanted her to feel limitless, confident, and that anything she set her mind to was possible. I had to get out of her way, but I also wanted to give her something of me so that wherever she is, if she needs me, I am there for her. When in doubt I draw, and out poured this little character—part-woman, part-child, part-animal, part-ninja. She became everything my imagination could aspire to. Her creation liberated me, and she flowed out of my pencil. She named herself Brave New Girl, and others nicknamed her BNG.

I kept drawing, and every day BNG popped out on the page fully formed, mid-adventure. Nothing held her back. If I got scared on a turbulent airplane flight, the next day BNG was riding the wings of an eagle. If I read an astronaut's autobiography (as you do), there she was floating about on the International Space Station peering down at Earth. When a bomb hurt Paris, she planted a garden of peace flowers. When I felt unconfident, she struck a power pose with penguins. I learned to reimagine my world with her antics. I learned to transform fear into fearlessness.

As I began posting the images online, women of all ages wrote to me saying, "I totally get her," "BNG is me!", "Go BNG!" BNG leapt out of me with her naïve squiggles, triangle dress, and stick legs. She's not a painting, as they say, but with her blank face we can all project ourselves onto her. We are her, and she is us. She shows us how to be tenacious; if she can't do something, she invents a way round it. If she's afraid, she challenges herself to move past fear and into courage. Through her we see that by using our imagination, our creativity, and our purpose, we can create a meaningful and happy life. In a scary world, she is the alternative to Superwoman, Wonder Woman, Tarzan, and James Bond. In her simple, non-show-offy, non-superhuman way, she does what she wants. And hurts no one by doing it.

One by one, the drawings took shape and BNG found her way to the publishers, who wove her exploits into this book. Insightful and timeless, it offers a humorous and inspiring path to fearlessness. Inside us all is a Brave New Girl just waiting to get out, and with every drawing, each page is an invitation to pause, reflect, smile, and take action. Now she not only accompanies me and Ruby May, but she's here for you too. You know, for those days when you hear yourself saying:

> *Why does life suck?*
> *Why is fear holding me back?*
> *Why do I feel so stressed out?*

In many ways life's not bad; you get through the day, feed yourself, keep a roof over your head, survive numerous sideswipes in the act of getting by. You're probably relatively successful and happy in many ways. But underneath lurks that negative voice that trips you up and holds you back. Fear stops you from being everything you want to be, from living abundantly with passion, freedom, and creativity. That annoying, persistent doubt scratching away with low-level anxiety, dread, and a sense of foreboding. Fear is one of the biggest causes of stress, which in turn is a major contributor to illness and disease. It doesn't have to be that way.

With BNG you can start to imagine being anything you want to be. You can change your story. When you feel anxious, fearful, frustrated, angry, or down in the dumps, just open the book to a random page and see what message Brave New Girl has for you. Carry the book with you; share it with friends and loved ones; enjoy its simple truths and wisdom. Then go out and be that Brave New Girl.

1

Aim for the moon

Be infinite

Reach for the stars

Make your way to the top

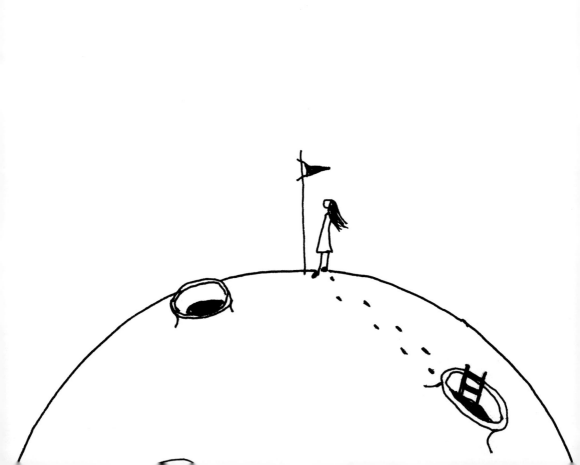

Make your mark

Be someone to watch

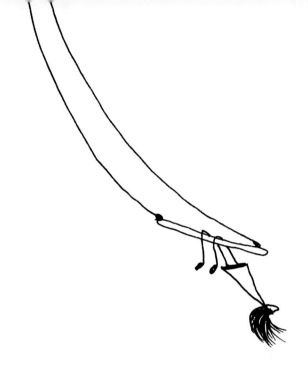

Try new tricks

Take risks

Only take the necessary precautions

Make a splash

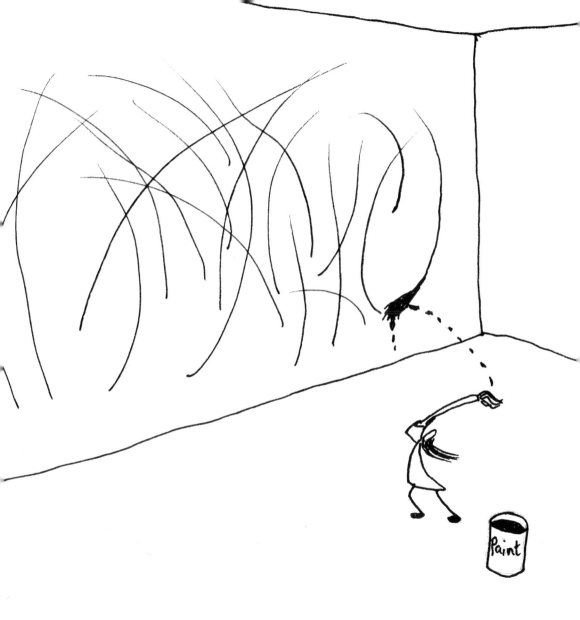

Launch yourself into the unknown

It starts with a seed

2

Face your

fears

When it's dark,
turn on the light

Practice self-defense

Enjoy the ride

Strengthen your shoulders

Scare away your bogeyman

Confront your demons

Power pose every morning

Learn the Maori haka

Put your inner dragon to good use

44

Don't be afraid of the past

3

Be your own

superhero

Know your own mind

Make it work your way

Take the road less traveled

Be intrepid

Stand your ground

Inspire others to follow

Know your own strength

Find someone to help you

Don't let anyone pull you down

Learn to take the spotlight

Step out from your hiding place

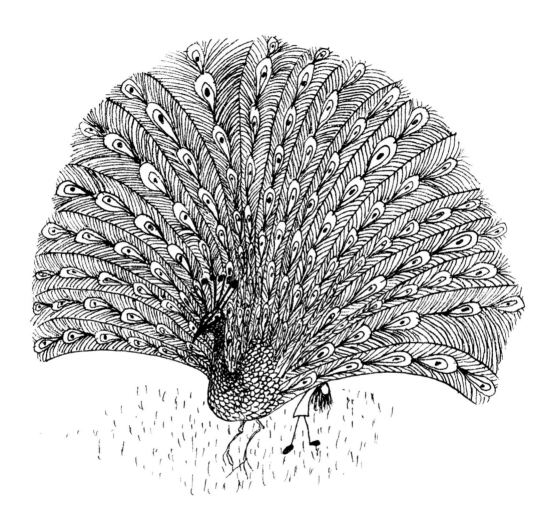

Be a force for good

4

~

Your time
will come

Make progress in small steps

Circle upward

Tenacity reaps rewards

Give it a good thwack

Pull some strings

Keep a lookout for opportunities

Be wary of pretty things

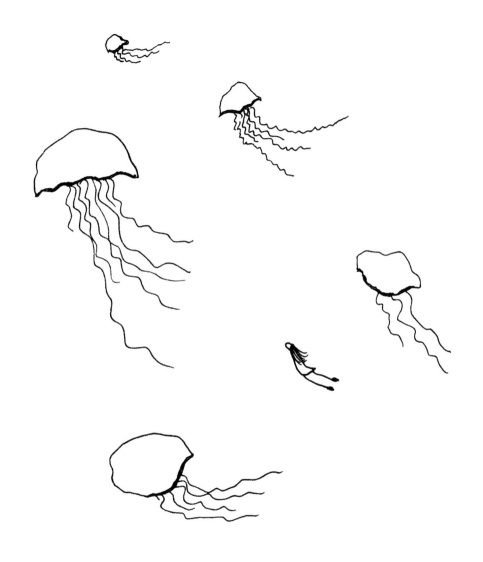

Persist in the face of resistance

Be flexible

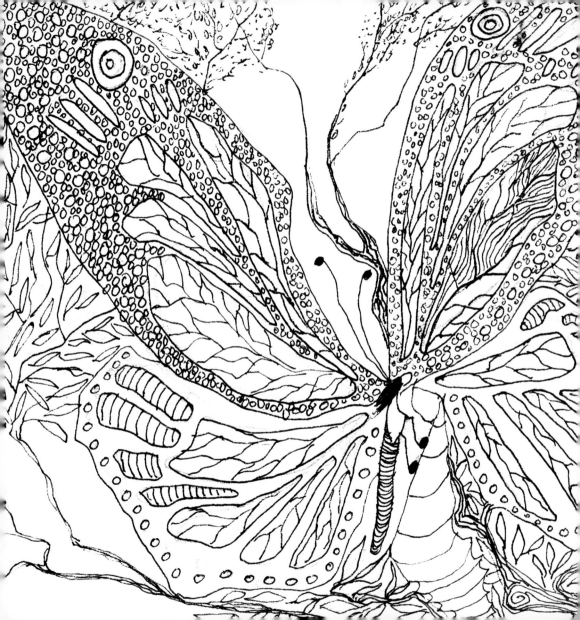

Reveal the true you

Give yourself the freedom to fail
and the liberty to learn

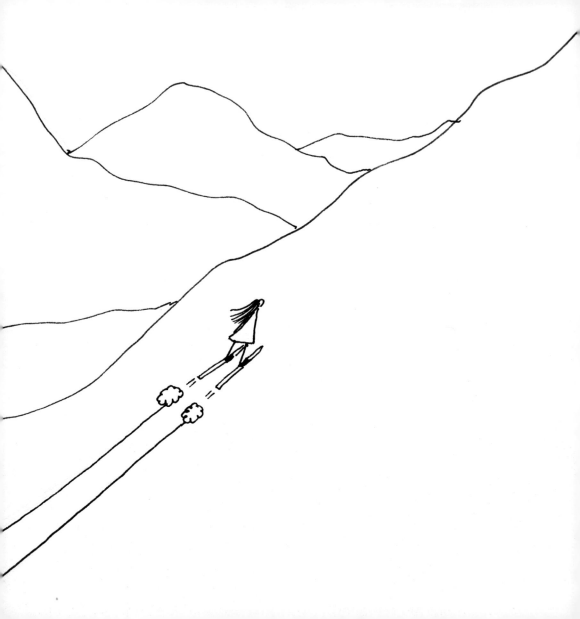

5

Reinvent the uphill struggle

Life's not always a breeze

Sometimes it's like pulling teeth

Unravel your problems one by one

Be prepared to do a lot
of firefighting

Learn to juggle
the ups with the downs

Embrace the loop-the-loop

Keep bad thoughts at bay

Search for the sunshine

Learn to love lemons

6

Look for

magic

Let your thoughts have wings

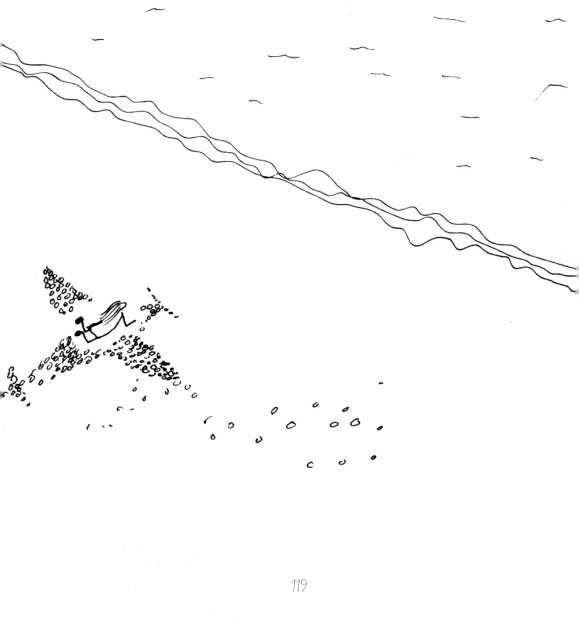

Take a trip to your
space station of imagination

Big dreams start in play

Spend part of each day
with your head in the clouds

Explore the mysteries
of other worlds

Run with the animal in you

Throw fairy dust at dark forces

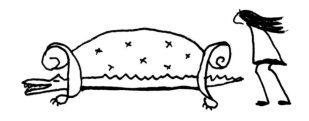

132

Look beneath the obvious

Challenge your mind

Try weird art stuff

Do your research

Learn from observation

7

Frivolity is freedom

Life's a doodle

Join in the festivities

Celebrate everything you can

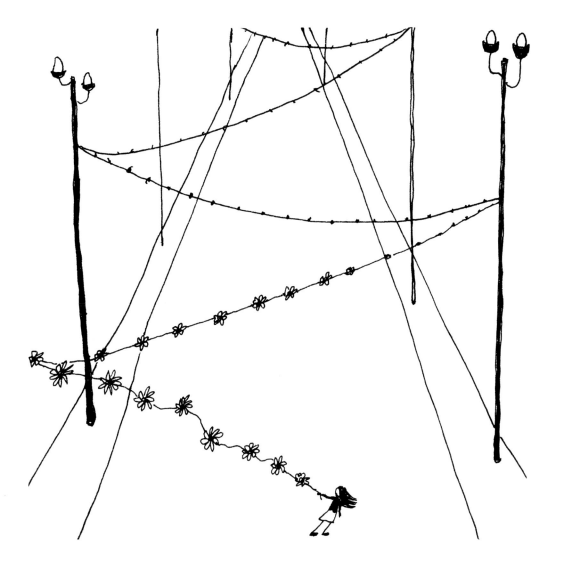

Learn to hula

Kick up some changes

154

Wild hats turn heads

Festoon your day with lights

8

Take a break

Sometimes it's okay to drift along

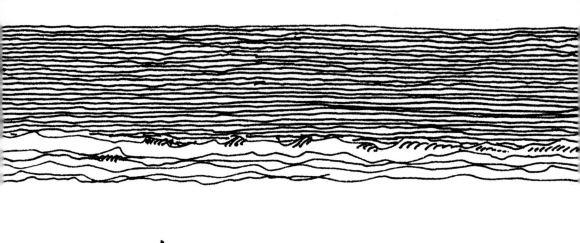

There is a time to be still

Find your peaceful place

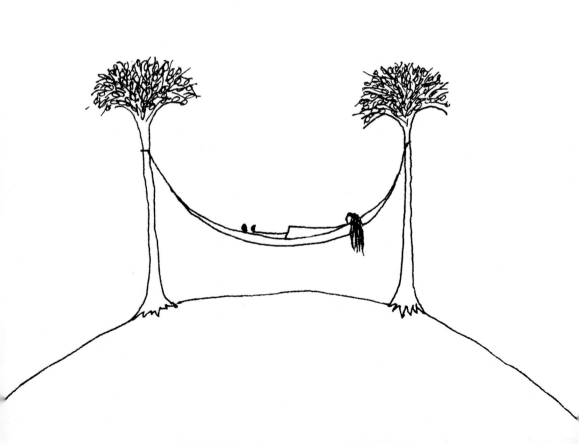

Patience is an art form

Good ideas need brewing

"No" is a complete sentence

Let wisdom carry you

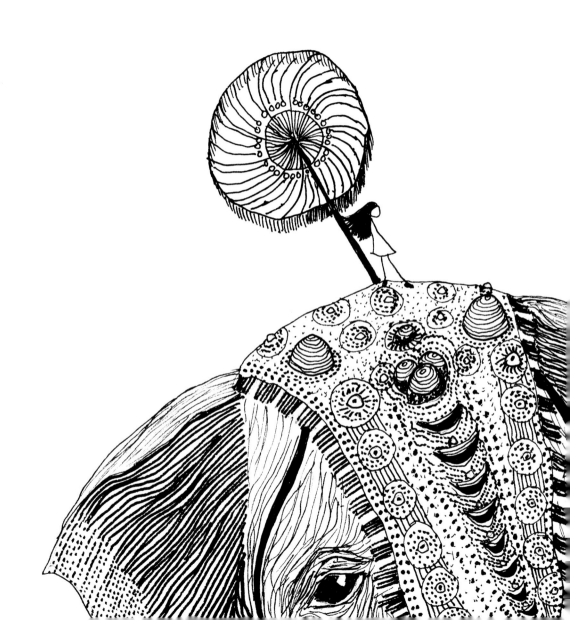

174

Call it a day

9

Work together
to achieve
great things

Together we can go places

Ride on the shoulders of giants

Talk to people

Ask your wise person for advice

Find someone to watch your back

Learn to trust

Recognize the needs of others

Spread the love

We don't always see eye to eye,
but we can try

Perform random acts of kindness

Create peaceful places everywhere

Karma comes back

Always offer an olive branch

Study the leaders

10

You're

good enough

Be the princess of your whole world

You can be ordinary and wonderful
at the same time

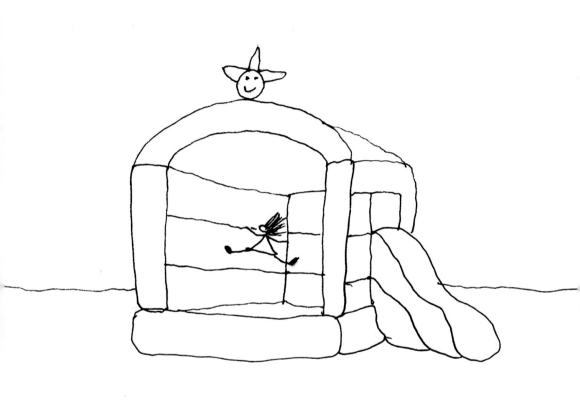

212

Perfection isn't fun

We all have our little surprises

Be happy in your own skin

Only give airtime to good thoughts

Be your biggest self

Do your own thing

Love yourself first

Acknowledgments

To my Mum and Dad, who have always supported and encouraged me to do what I love; to Pablo for his love, 100 percent belief, and boundless cheerleading; to Tobe for his unfailing friendship and co-parenting partnership; to my dear friends and family for being amazing human beings—compassionate, kind, courageous, curious, outrageous, funny, anarchic, creative, caring, talented, inspiring, wine-loving, impulsive, intuitive, gutsy, ballsy, and unbreakable. Having you all out there is the best. To my pencil, you make me laugh when I see what comes out of you; to my eraser for hiding my hiccups; and to my pen for making something out of the odd stuff in my head. To my passionate agent Clare Conville, who swept BNG off her feet and took me under her wing. To my wonderful publisher Amanda Harris, editorial assistant Lucy Haenlein, publicist Virginia Woolstencroft, and the whole team at Orion Spring who have been so awesomely creative in bringing the book to life in such a magical way. A big noisy thank-you to you all, from the bottom of my heart and the top of BNG's lungs. We wouldn't be here without you.

About the author

Lou Hamilton is an artist, author, and life coach. Lou has two children and lives on an island surrounded by water in London. She has a rowing boat and an allotment, cycles everywhere, and swims outside when she dares. She is addicted to books and loves shopping, traveling, movies, art exhibitions, drawing, painting, writing, and working with women who want to fear less and be more. You can visit her and BNG at www.BraveNewGirl.co.uk.